THE AUTHOR, Karen Gemma Brewer, is an award-winning
writer, poet and performer from Ceredigion in west Wales.
Her work combines emotion and mundanity with a strong
sense of the absurd. In addition to her own work she has
edited books by other Wales-based writers.

More
Scarecrow

Than
Pirate

Karen Gemma Brewer

MOSAÏQUEPRESS

First published in 2025

MOSAÏQUE PRESS
Registered office:
Bank Gallery, High Street
Kenilworth, Warwickshire
CV8 1LY

Series editor: John Eliot

ISBN 978-1-906852-24-5

To Patrick, Annabelle and Tim
great characters, writers and friends
you live on in your words and works
but we miss you all the same

Contents

The author is greatly indebted to the editors, publishers and organisers who commission and publish her work and book her for performances and workshops.

'Ysbryd Bywyd' and 'Spirit of Life' were published in *Ruby Tuesdays – an anthology by Lampeter Writers' Workshop* (Peter Bridge & Steffan, 2024)

'Whirled Peas' is published in *Peaceweavers – an anthology for peace and justice* (Culture Matters, 2025)

'A Day In Aberaeron' was first published in *Correnti Incrociate 4* (Mosaïque Press, 2024) in English and Italian

'DividEND' is published in *We Not Me/Ni Nid Fi – an anthology of Radical Poetry from Contemporary Wales* (Culture Matters, 2025)

'Dog & Stick' was first published in *Ruby Tuesdays* (2024)

'Shoe to Kill' is published in *Red Poets 31 – Radical poetry from Wales and the world* (Red Poets, 2025)

A version of 'Ill wind III' titled 'Ill Wind' appeared in *Seeds From A Dandelion* (Cowry Publishing, 2017) and a second version 'Another Ill Wind' in *Dancing In The Sun* (Cowry Publishing, 2022)

'Myplace' was first published in *Curente La Rascruce 2* (Mosaïque Press, 2024) in English and Romanian

Foreword
Geraint Lewis, writer and actor

Having enjoyed Karen Gemma Brewer's previous volumes of poetry, *dancing in the sun* and *Seeds from a dandelion* I felt a great privilege but also slight trepidation when I was asked to write a foreword for her latest collection. Within minutes my nervousness disappeared, metamorphosing into wonder and laughter, safe in the hands or rather voice of someone at ease with her craft.

I read some of the poems on my iPhone during my daily walk along the banks of the river Aeron. I laughed out loud on so many occasions I was beginning to get bewildered looks from dogs as well as their owners. That's the beauty of laughter. It's an honest arbiter. You can't cheat it. It comes literally from the guts.

Karen's love of words is infectious. She plays with them like toys, often with hilarious consequences. Trump's Supreme Court morphs into a 'chicken supreme court' ('Bananas'); courting an amoeba (yes, you read that correctly) her unusual beau gets to know her 'from my top to mitosis' before they are pronounced 'wife and lowest form of life' ('Bug Love').

Her comic gift isn't limited to puns. Sometimes she juxtaposes words which make you sit up almost in a jolt, marvelling at the originality. Who else but Karen would put 'séance' before 'sandwiches' ('A Meeting of Caterpillars') or 'Crematory' before 'Clowns' ('Crematory Clowns')?

Under the absurdity and hyperbole some serious themes are explored, often in a visceral way that takes the reader by surprise. These include global warming, the hypocrisy of religion, the corrosiveness of social media, the intrinsic greed of capitalism, genocide. Even here the juxtaposing of words is used to striking effect. For example, we are accustomed to seeing the word 'singing' after 'children' not 'children singeing' and in the same poem there is a sinister

9

tone as the humour is darkened by the realities of war – 'To accompaniment of lyres truth runs by with pants on fire' ('Whirled Peas' – itself a pun on world peace).

· I won't dwell too much on Karen's use of images, just let you enjoy them, with the warning that some of them will take your breath away. I particularly liked 'awaiting the moon and a hillside Turkey to wed us' ('A Sticky Situation').

We also get a charming sense of the poet's affinity for Wales, possibly best captured in the poem 'Film Plots and Titles if Quentin Tarantino was Welsh', my favourites being 'A Swansea man sunbathing on Mumbles beach – Jack y Brown' and 'One village, Two chapels – Pulpit Friction.'

As a fellow inhabitant of Ceredigion I was particularly fond of Karen's acute sense of place. 'Grannell' is a moving poem about the river she has known for decades, a tribute to a tributary as it were. It is also a great example of how the poet gets us straight into the poem, without any fuss –

> In night still summer your giggle lulls me
> though our beds are two fields apart.

This particular poem shows that Karen is also a high calibre nature poet, drawing on her hands-on agricultural background, a background on which she ponders as she marks her move from her farm to town,

> a few seconds of tears shed on your bank, Grannell Field
> a last weep before my sweep from farm to a town by the
> sea.

Nature poetry is particularly relevant in the age of global warming. 'Ysbryd Bywyd' is a poem of thanks and of praise to a way of life that one senses Karen has herself lived. It is a beautiful tribute to the simple but satisfying cycle of rural life on the land in Ceredigion. It is no coincidence that this heartfelt, timeless piece is the one poem that Karen has chosen to include in both languages ('Spirit of Life / Ysbryd Bywyd').

In the past Karen has cited Spike Milligan and Max Boyce as influences. In her shorter poems I feel she sometimes reaches Emily Dickinson-type depths of concise ambiguity. Her nature writing, a harshness underpinned with a surprising tenderness, is sometimes reminiscent of RS Thomas, though all distilled of course through Karen's unique voice.

You can surely sense by now that the sheer variety of poems within this volume is astounding. Some poems are completely in dialogue. One, 'Blew', is only thirteen words (but…well, blew my mind). Others, to feel their true effect, must be sung. Which brings us to the tension, a delightful one, between the spoken or sung word and the written or read one. If you get a chance please try and see Karen live. With her deadpan delivery, perfect rhythm and timing, her readings add another dimension to an already enjoyable experience.

The bewildered dog walkers on the banks of the river Aeron should buy this book to satisfy their curiosity. They should read the poems aloud to their dogs or better still let the dogs read them too. For in Karen's enchantingly exuberant universe, where short-nosed elephants go on a day out to Aberaeron and 'caterpillars of power' hold important meetings at The Savoy and amoebae get married, surely our canine friends can read?

Normal words don't really do justice to *More Scarecrow Than Pirate*. In the spirit of the book I will venture to say I found it guffawesome. I'm sure you will too.

More Scarecrow Than Pirate

If I could only buckle my swash
polish my cutlass, patch in my *i*
might I be dashing, debonair and daring
a leader, a feeder of socialist change?
More scarecrow than pirate.

In dreams I'm always buccaneer brave
swinging in rigging, avast ye, ahoy!
Truth finds me pointing, wide-eyed and legless
a fielder not wielder, no queen of the seize.
More scarecrow than pirate.

Our cause from the nest in a dead woman's chest
blow the crow down with all hands on deck
repel all hoarders, hornswogglers, malfeasors
haul away me charities don't abandon our wreck.

All I can offer stories and verse
drawing no cutlass, just a straw short
my stake in the ground a shivering timber
I'm minstrel with installed revolution pause.
More scarecrow than pirate.

Lost Without a Trace

Plenty of zinc in my diet
I suck on the corners of corrugated sheets
galvanise on the wing
wear hobnail stilettoes
vault railings to swing up the slide
iron bullets
nail fingers on fishes
spend a copper or two on the side
I've got cartoon legs
and Manga knees
run like colours
pant like genies
nick all their wishes
for my magic market stall
easy pick lock
they never cobalt the door
find me Wednesdays and Saturdays
selenium all
but don't expect a free lunch
I owe the diner a haul
built quite a reputation
though I'm not one to chrome
a magnetic personality
will always find home
suggest you never test my metal
eaten what I've become
life is never boron
when you're Molly B Done

Prince Pince Nez

The Prince of Wales' Bridge
exists to stop his glasses
sliding down his face

Ysbryd Bywyd

Ceredigion - tir glas, rhos a mynydd
Ceredigion - ei ffin Teifi a'r môr
Ceredigion - ffermio a barddoniaeth
Ceredigion - cartre ysbryd bywyd

aredig y cae, taenu'r calch
hau yr hedyn, dychwelyd tail
torri'r gwair, medi'r yd
llenwi'r sgubor, cwblhau'r cylch
molwch y glaw, addoli'r haul
byddwch yn un â'r wlad hon

godro'r fuwch, wyna y famog
casglu'r wyau, bwydo'r moch
trwsio'r ffens, hongian y gât
plannu'r goeden, gosod y clawdd
hyfforddi ceffyl, farchogaeth y bryn
byddwch yn un â'r wlad hon

adnabod yr adar, goglais brithyll
gweld y dwrgi, winc i'r llwynog
dewis y fadarch, blasu'r perlysiau
gwasgu'r afal, mwynhewch y blodau
cyfri'r sêr, wafo i'r lleuad
byddwch yn un â'r wlad hon

Spirit of Life

Ceredigion – grassland, rhos and mountain
Ceredigion – bordered by Teifi and sea
Ceredigion – farming and poetry
Ceredigion – home to the spirit of life

plough the field, spread the lime
sow the seed, return manure
mow the hay, reap the crop
fill the barn, complete the circle
praise the rain, worship the sun
be one with this land

milk the cow, lamb the ewe
collect the eggs, feed the pigs
hang the gate, mend the fence
plant the tree, lay the hedge
train the horse, ride the hill
be one with this land

spot the birds, tickle the trout
see the otter, wink to the fox
pick the mushroom, taste the herbs
crush the apple, enjoy the flowers
count the stars, wave to the moon
be one with this land

Truth Hole

Is freedom found
in release of secrets
do seven magpies make
black and white tart
unsavoury end
to an unseen start
a stolen prize
hearts apart.

Old Money

Penny for your thoughts
Ha'penny for your dreams
Farthing for your loyalty
Florin for the Queen
Half a crown change to Spare
Thruppenny bitter sing
Silver sea of sixpences
Pound against the King
Who'll pay Prince of Wales' Bill
More than a few bob Owain
Crown for Cymru's water vale
Cofiwch Dreweryn

Crematory Clowns (Advertisement)

Want to bring a beaming smile
to the face of broken hearted
mix peals of laughter amongst the bells
as if the corpse had farted
worried that the after do
might be deader than the departed
need some flare to get this party started
Crazy World of Arthur Brown on the turntable
just make a call to Crematory Clowns
and put the fun back into funeral

To have the eulogy pronounced
while breathing helium from a balloon
coffin bearers mimic the lope of baboons
to the Funky Gibbon tune
a plaintive voice echo from inside
"it's awfully dark in this room"
instead of hearing Jones the voice croon
to be loved is not unusual
just make that call to Crematory Clowns
and put the fun back into funeral

Leading the cortege our horn will beep
Tequilla, Dixie, La Cucaracha
then every mile our hearse backfires
when the doors and boot blow off
with rainbow smoke creating haze
so mourners weep and cough
we pitch our humour hard and soft
specialise in the impuberal
so make that call to Crematory Clowns
and put the fun back into funeral

For supply of caskets with large red noses
that squeak when squeezed and glow in the dark
strategically positioned fireworks
that rocket up the chimney at cremation's spark
personalised accoutrements
neon headstone with the jaws of a shark
giant replica head of a pet dog, with barks
to be worn superhumeral
who ya gonna call" but Crematory Clowns
who put the fun back into funeral.

That's Something

Things are looking up
we're not quite there
but almost on the cusp
moving on from living on
Charley Farley's rusk

I won't ever go to war
that's something
or scratch my slogans on your wall
that's something

When bighead buys a hat
excitement builds
and fills up to the brim
feel the fear that death is near
Dante's antonym

I don't have to lock the door
that's something
or mop your body from the floor
that's something

A monkey or a bear
who gets your vote
to lead us to the brink
nothing sound to hand-me-down
mushroom push-room blink

Even running water roars
that's something
and contracts always come with claws
that's something

Won't kill ourselves today
watching paint dry
like blood splashed on the wall
lines and curls that spell out words
slow gun motion pall

Finish line on sandy shore
that's something
medals rust in heroes' craw
that's something
things are looking up

Old, Fashioned

I live in an old, fashioned place
where trees are made of wood
houses of stone
hearts of flint and flame.

Where roads wriggle
from Aberaeron to Llanbedr Pont Steffan
Llandysul and Tregaron
Aberystwyth to Aberteifi.

Where white/grey smudges
of half-bred sheep
bleat on green
fescued Cambrians.

Where cliffs dash
along pebble beaches
crash in a dolphined sea
seagulls on chips.

Where tongues twist
around two languages
ales sour
if we drank too slow.

Where song is air
poetry light
story blood
bound only in music.

Where history
is memory
earth soul
gladness Gwlad.

A Meeting of Caterpillars

I attended a meeting of caterpillars
One afternoon at the Savoy
We had tea and séance sandwiches
Soar the butter fly
Our chairman was an Admiral
from the Russian Fleet
Brown was there with Glanville
Green, Marsh, Wood and White
plus to maintain the chrysalist
the grand old Duke of Burgundy
men once caterpillars of power
who fritillaried it all away.

Whirled Peas

Like a bird's eye on barbed wire
swung in circles high and higher
holding steady, almost ready
one, two, three

Bricks to dust the droning choir
deserts gifts of Mother Gaia
no more planting just dismantling
river and sea

Missile tows in kiss goodbyer
genocide by sideshow crier
general whingeing, children singeing
incensory

Safety zones slightly less dire
advertised by sky-dropped flyer
almost moving town disroofing
on TV

To accompaniment of lyres
truth runs by with pants on fire
leaders wisely close their eyes
so they don't see

Heady heights which to aspire
all decked out in fine attire
crosswire sights inhuman rights
inaccuracies

No journalist gets to enquire
banned or bombed unless complier
broken story floored and flawy
demockracy

No pure race just jambalaya
destination always via
answer only minestrone
whirled peas

Bug Love

I've fallen in love with an amoeba
for speed of thought it is the placebo
we met when I went for a drink that time
brandy and coke with a dash of slime
I'll always remember our very first kiss
your diamond smile, such a (Petri) dish
no touching hands sweet *Chaos carolinense*
a prescription from the love dispensary

My friends all said I was a fool
but you taught me how to divide and drool
discarding all their pleasantries
placarding all with dysentery
delighted to be your Desdemona
as you held me in your pseudopoda
by polypoidal proto-plasma flow
to our osmosis oasis vacuole

From my top to mitosis, sinus to snout
you've got to know me inside out
investigating every little fact
even read my intestinal tract
till it was time to stop being single-cell
plight our troth at the wishing well
Administer: "I now pronounce you wife
and the lowest form of life."

"You may now kiss the nucleotide."

Shore Leave

Take a walk along the shore
toes touching the tide
feet against the grain of sands
salty taste of brine
rockpool smells seaweed and shells
throaty seagull cries
there was nothing else you could've said
would've made Death change her mind

Gull has flown
wave has rolled
sun has sunken
in your sorrow

Haul away rigged memories
shanties out of time
pirate pictures hero words
seven scenes sublime
eyes ablaze in salient glaze
pebble dreams' wet shine
nothing else you could've done
to make Death change her mind

Lull has blown
bell has tolled
sun has risen
somewhere tomorrow

A Day in Aberaeron

My friend keeps short-nosed elephants
and takes them out for walks
held to heel on leads of cerebral bleeds
and occasional treats of chalk

They stroll along the promenade
whenever the tide pulls in
cursing the monks who bred out their trunks
as they'd love to wade in for a swim

They settle for removing their shoes and socks
and wiggling their toes in the stones
though it gives them a rash like pebble dash
it oils the slide of their life trombones

They rarely lay out for a suntan
thick skin remains saggy and grey
dressed in wide brimmed hats, sunshades and cravats
in a look that seems far-far away

I can never quite tell what they're thinking
though their manners are always tip-top
I've somehow suspected they're a mite disconnected
and if ever they start would it stop?

With their paddles and wiggles completed
my friend snaps them back on their leads
and pushing a trolley with their poo-bags and brollies
heads in search of a nice place to eat

We're endowed in colourful Aberaeron
with premises elephant-friendly
they pick the one with wide chairs even though it's upstairs
order Te Cymraeg with a bamboo cream sundae

After tea and a snooze by the harbour
they watch the sun set in Cardigan Bay
then with minimal fuss catch the last T5 Bus
and reminisce on their Aberaeron day

Lime Regis

You may have heard on the Edinburgh Fringe
like repetitive squeals of an unoiled door hinge
or extracting fresh blood with an oral syringe
that nothing at all in the world rhymes with orange

The queen crowns her breakfast with Marmalade on toast
as a means to deflect dissenters and jeers
she discovered one slice to each side of the head
means a nice quiet ride if she Adajamir.
Take care when online Kawachi Bankan
make certain you always Kanpei
or they'll play Balady hell, perhaps sound your death Nell
lock you up, throw the Key Lime away.
Know when to Shaddock and keep Shangjuan
especially if Shonan Gold
word gets around you've Jabara
they'll Pomelo your chest 'til you fold .
Don't stand for any Mangshanyegan
tell Haruka to just Bergermot
avoid all the risk of a Citron arrest
as for sure they won't ever Kumquat.
You'll rarely find Grapefruit to be grateful
the Lemon 24hrs zest grater
but never go pandering for Mandarin
they'll catch you Satsuma or later.
If perchance Buddha's Hand Tangerine
take a breath, try your best to stay Seville
don't respond with a wild Florentine
please smile sweet, don't explete the full Kinnow.
Should you appear Anadomikan boudoir
with First Lady lying in bed
ignore her requests to Clymenia
or they likely might Koji your head.
Corsican do whatever Yuzu
take the pith or a cruise on the rind
king or queen your appeal has its limit
oh my darling always Clementine.

Cause for Crows

I could murder a worm sandwich
Raindance on the lawn
carry water
pop pebbles into milk bottles
march with my majorette baton
dangle snails from a balcony
be mistook for a rook
I could murder a worm
bombard with pinecones
hold a funeral
nest on a tall ship
cause a sound effect
play drums on Ænima
appear ravenous
I could murder

Fear to Hope

Living in this garden of FEAR
Apple and a smile a daily FEAT
I bake bread then kill the MEAT
Feed the snake lying in the MOAT
Sandwich red in flesh it likes MOST
Lay out gingham play my part as HOST
Swing my picnic fork and stab that HOSE
Pinned tight to the ground I leave in HOPE

Lash

The hand that held the belt
had a conductor's swing
brought percussion
and me into hand
a symphony of cries
pain and surprise
you never played
this hand before
or again.

Grannell

In night still summer your giggle lulls me
though our beds are two fields apart
and there's barely enough of you to separate parishes
I can step stone from Llanwenog to Llanarth
leap to Llanfihangel Ystrad (or is it Dihewyd now?)
all those empty churches that don't belong
heaped upon pagan lands to drain our bogs of silver.
We run together a half-life, from my XXs to LXs
while you erode Roman concrete for centuries.
No gold below remnants of their bridge to Troedyrhiw
but blue jewelled Kingfishers dive bombing minnows
from a tree at the Rhos. I hop, skip, jump across trout
too fly for a fly, sucker to a tickle and a sizzle in my pan.
You send otters up the brook that skirts Bottom Field,
divides Stream Field, to the stone pit where a wheel span
your power through iron rods twisting in cast pipes that lie
beneath Glyn Yr Helyg's cobbles, now turning only to rust.
In spring you rage against my tractor, the only means to cross
drown lambs who follow stupid mothers into your torrent
laugh with me at rogue ewe Danu, who dives your depths,
surfaces to greener grass on Pont Marchog's side of the fence.
In 2023 you bore 2,424 hours of Cribyn sewage to the Teifi
plus a few seconds of tears shed on your bank, Grannell Field
a last weep before my sweep from farm to a town by the sea.

Noisy Lorry Driver

I don't remember his name
what he looked like
or even who he drove for
though he was a regular visitor.
We knew him as 'Noisy Lorry Driver'
something about his tone and manner.
He seemed pleasant enough
but when he arrived, every time
the cows would shit themselves.
Ever heard a herd of cows
crap together in a concrete yard?
Dollops of green custardy shite
dropped from a height of four feet plus.
Clap, clap, clap, clap, clap.
First one cow, then several, then 20, then 100
legs planted, tails raised, no synchronisation
just a multitude of unhappy, clappy, crappy, splats
their unity view in a community poo.
When spending a penny put thought on pause
there's not always acclaim in a round of applause

Examination

Clock ticks echo as the hands creep round
slowly, oh so slowly, time seeps by
a heart full of song but I can't make a sound
tongue turning numb as my throat croaks dry

It's nearly 3pm. It'll soon be time
people are still writing, can they be so slow?
Perhaps they're composing their own short rhymes
or trying to remember what they don't know

Quarter of an hour still to wait
heavy feels time as I pen these words
speed up clock, add a gallop to your gait
I'm wasting away encaged like a bird

Time's up at last, I'm ready to fly free
quick, collect the papers and let me out
to do what I want to do, be who I want to be
to run and jump and sing and dance and shout, **shout, shout!**

Free Peace Sweet

Authority turns easily to tyranny
inequality steals freedom from poverty
wealthy abide in the law

Find your self
Find your place
Find your peace

Love hertz
heart sparks
blown ohm

Wondering

Wonder what it would be like to be a badger
who's sent to fox school, mastering the art of fitting in,
badgered badger buys brown balaclava,
remember Nan knitting grey overhead wool,
everything except the eyes, no fooling,
disguise an idiot, big ears red warm, irritated,
laughing kids pointing, hidden face reddening,
initially sheepish then fists flailing, head ramming,
raw knuckles sore in embarrassment blush,
itchy as balaclava neck, itchy as an unshorn sheep
scratching against brush, snagging fleece on fences,
and trees, barb-wired tufts flagging the countryside,
flocks taunting shepherds washing holey socks, darn it
can you knit a hijab?

Wonder how woodworm party
in their sawdusted labyrinth behind the piano's strings,
bunting, lightshow, white wine spritzers, sticks-on-sausages,
Time to Fly on pink and blue helium filled balloons,
couples in unison doing the Bump, Twist and Fox-Wiggle,
no quick-stepping on toes, white lines and purple rain,
last sand dance against the grain, kids laughing and pointing
at floor and ceiling in the fever of Saturday night
before flight-hole entry to a wider universe, leaving me
on the other side of the door, sitting on a hallway floor,
head against carpet, eyes closed, ears pounding
to disco bass and blame, lost in confusion of disinvitation,
when you worm your way in, do they always
make you crawl home?

Wonder if toads get a frog in the throat
when they bullhorn croaks through disallowed speakers
to crowd seeker's, lily pad sneakers, sleepers and seepers,
hoppers and leapers, screamers and bleepers,
chirpers and cheepers, nattering Jack-in-the-box creekers,
Uncle Tom peepers, grim poison dart reapers,
inlanded marshian give me the creepers, shut that door,
je t'adore, worldwide webbed feet, legs folded neatly
in a boîte à déjeuner, swamped, span out of hand, with
no chance to take a grand stand, needlessly kneeless
prey-du-jour, tell it raw, boil to the core, toad or frog
am I just a bump on a log in a bog, a Darwinian tad poll,
truthful or amphibian, waiting to be towed
all the way to oblivion?

DividEND

Can a land be divided
other than by mountain, river, lake or sea
or is it always divided
by lines drawn on paper and in minds
can a land be divided
by colour, race, gender, tongue and creed
can a land be divided
by mitre, kippah, turban, hijab, bindi
can a land be divided
by money, caste, class, clan, old school tie
can a land be divided
by health, age and disability
can a land be divided
by wall, fence, rampart, ditch and dyke
can a land be divided
by who you love or how you choose to die
can a land be divided
by teacher, preacher, politician, king
can a land be divided
by flag, anthem, oath and uniform
can a land be divided
by superpowers pulling puppet strings
can a land be divided
by stone, club, rifle, tank and bomb
can a land be divided
by truth, lies, connectivity
can a land be divided
by drug, bribe, dam or mine
can a land be divided
other than by mountain, river, lake or sea
or is it always divided
by lines drawn on paper and in minds
must a land be divided
or can a land be shared?

Film Plots and Titles if Quentin Tarantino was Welsh

Plot	Title
Ferry stories	Once Upon a Time in Holyhead
England's rugby pack	The Hateful Eight
Sianco sells all his shops but one	Sianco Unchained
Sir Thomas Picton and Richard Pennant	Inglorious Basterds
Wearing ear plugs and defenders on the glass bottle recycling run	Deaf Proof
Mole catcher's invoice	Kill Bill
A Swansea man sunbathes on Mumbles beach	Jack Y Brown
One village, Two chapels	Pulpit Friction
Six north Walians at Treweryn	Reservoir Gogs

Dog & Stick

I thought I would poke
the dog in our yard
with my pointy stick

I knew it would bite
it wasn't asleep
but poked anyway

When bitten before
someone always came
to drag it away

It yelps at my stab
angrily attacks
rescuers arrive

But why do they watch
it tear me apart
get it off, get off ....

Haicuckoo

Backwards ukiah
Japanese ukulele?
Shape and Formby

Thick Skinned

Bright yellow birds, aviary bred.
Not canaries, yet still the gas kills them.

Under a blazing sun their bodies dry
on terracotta roof tiles,
like rows of fried, rectangular, bird yolk blood eggs.

Donkey powered machinery grinds
dried cadavers to bright yellow powder,
captured in cardboard stumps,
labelled 'Instant Custard'.

Love You Again

Gathering my pollen
you said I'll always be your flower
I thought we had stamen power
what a blooming fool.

The sweet taste of my nectar
was not enough for you
touched another flower or two
petals gold to blue.

I could never ever love you again.

Don't ever call me honey
the memories are just too raw
hexagons are out the door
set my style askew.

You buzz by every morning
perform your please forgive me dance
beg me for a second chance
go and wax your brood.

I could never ever love you again.

Always thought that I'd go far
but I can't get out of bed
put my dreams on you instead
and away they flew

I'm a self-appraising flower
and can see my summer's gone
far too late to right what's wrong
you were not bee true

I will never ever feel love again.

Bananas

USA land of the dreaming free
fell for a Republican pelican
and Donald was his name – Bananas
One dark day they dissolved moral codes
and let him run for President
and to bend laws as he chose
Oh

Clownishly criminal Donald Trump
can swing his tongue like a golf club
so narcissistically self-absorbed
Trump, Trump, Trump – Bananas
Pompously pumped up an orange gump
yet ringmaster at the White House
truth and fiction forever entwined
Trump, Trump, Trump – Bananas

Republican Party calling all pull the chain
to flush away compassion and rights
on the road to big pay days – Bananas

Right by right women marginalised
with Donald leaking the masquerade
as power glints his eyes – Bananas
At his word the chicken supreme court
gave him total immunity
turning felony to sport
Oh

Fascist delusional Donald Trump
can bring the world to a death stop
so ignoble a hate filled slob
Trump, Trump, Trump – Bananas
Odiously oafish a cruel chump
Americans on a knife edge
Cosmic Horizon for minorities
Trump, Trump, Trump – Bananas

Name Calling

"Have you got a bookmark?"
she chirps
worried about dogears
as I extract a volume
from our boxroom library

"Breakfast will be ready shortly!"
she shouts
up our dogleg staircase
as I succumb to pillows
for an extra five minutes

"I'll be back soon!"
she hollers
heading doggedly
in search of provisions
while I listen to radio

Will I be named afresh
I wonder
dog days of December
after Mark, Shortly and Soon
new name for a virgin year

Virginia is not her name
I muse
mid-afternoon snooze
assured there will be one
in memory's periphery

Shoe Kazoo

Walking the river trail to Lover's Bridge
I saw two trees hold hands
pretend to be a forest
gather nuts and bark
a lost glove on a hand stand
an ant pumping weights
footprints and pine art
and a dead bird that hummed
no wood bears or porridge
no goldielocked gates
just travel in style crooked and sharp.
My Samsung streams river songs
bedrock and stepping stone roses,
ducks quark through upturned noses
particular with their Rs
point to Sky with their arse
beckon with eggs
surf the web through their toeses
beg to be fed crumbs of death
the best thing before sliced bread
all my ducks in a death row death throe
what's up ducks either down or dead.
Frogs croak, giving up on hip-hop
choke out an ominous drill
808 bass in a race to a new place
legless in France kick off a trap dance
the bitterest PiL a virgin ever swallowed
tongues like party horns, kazoos in their shoes
feathers in leathers from the greens to the blues.

Indian Rubber necked cormorant
balanced on a corpulent naan
silently chants a korma rant
raises wing skirts' shadowy flirt
to lure dishy fishy corporate shoal
in range of plunging non de plume dive
trout down the throat wriggling whole
stickleback karma devoured alive.
Looping my loop I see on return
that nuptial forest upright and firm
hold out their branches call "Halt!" to the wind
like a new Twm Sion Catti shouting "Stand and Rescind!"
from the overtaking lane of the A55.

Being Human

Dear Mum,
thanks for the card and cake – mmm….
All going krill so far,
came top in *Rage* yesterday,
second in *Bullying*
and am in the first quartile
for *Humour & Depression*.

Still struggling
with *Discrimination* though,
such an alien concept
I can't quite put my
tentacle on it.

Teach says not to worry
as very few students
even graduate
with any real grasp
and I'm doing so well
with everything else.

Teach says,
if I carry on at the rate I'm going,
I'll easily make the top 10%
that get to do their middle term
actually on the planet!
Hopefully
in the parliamentary group.

Anyway,
got to sloop,
nearly time for zquisch.
I'm playing up front today
so takes twice as long
to get changed.
Will post this on the way.
So pleased you persuaded me
to read *Humanities*.

love to Pop,
Treen xx

Piggy Bop

More than a bacon rasher
I have pride at my side
a guide to stop any backslides
I see them grab their piece of the pie
all those fingers in all those pies
I hear the death buzz of blowflies

More than a bacon rasher
outside of the glass
all the doors and windows are tight
no chance the truth leaks in tonight
as oligarchs dance power high
riding on algorithmic lies
and every star looks close tonight

Snorting
oink oink, oink oink, oinky oink oink
oink oink, oink oink, oinky oink oink
oink oink, oink oink, oinky oink oink, oink oink

All locked in our cars
sliced into bacon rashers
joyride even if we don't like
seething cities writhe inside
won't see the gas float in the sky
just drill the golden baby dry
the stars seem so close tonight

Oh the bacon rasher
How now she cries
all the bacon rashers
they cry and they cry
Who controls your window
and what you see
deaf to the screaming in the sky
blinded by stars so close tonight
mute to the children ripped aside
lame to the acid ocean dive
And all of this was down to you and me
in every pie now all the fingers bleed
crypto-maniacs' capital seed
so bacon rashers ride and see what's mine

Snorting
oink oink, oink oink, oinky oink oink
oink oink, oink oink, oinky oink oink
oink oink, oink oink, oinky oink oink, oink oink

I'm just a bacon rasher

Shoe to Kill

There was an old woman
who lived in a shoe
she had so many children
but only got tax credit on the first two.
Her landlords refused
to do up the laces
and hiked up her rent
'til she was forced to change places
then let by the night
on airsole B&B
to tourists who fancied
a cute boot in the country.

There was an old woman
who lived on the streets
her children in care
learning new tricks for sweets.
She stood on the corner
bundled up with *Big Issue*
which she waved at her landlords
who told her to "Shoo!"

Owl and Dove

Owl doesn't work backwards
even in Welsh
no reverse gear
so when she hoots
get out of the way.
Dove is a bird of letters
one not even in the alphabet
yet
later than Jay.
Owl,
brass feathered for brassy weather.
Dove,
a pearl in her mother's shell.
An undynamic duo
no underpants under or over
their cut-loose tights.
Two posh birds doubly meant
all plumage and no knickers·
beneath each other's wing.
Duende.

MacDonald Had a Gallery

MacDonald had a gallery
Caravaggio
the gallery displayed Van Gogh
Caravaggio
with an ear, ear 'ere
and an ear, ear there
'ere an ear, there an ear
everywhere an ear, ear
MacDonald had a gallery
Caravaggio

Culporter Conspiracy

"Someone comes."

"Not this early, you must have spot-eye."

"Look for yourself, if you can undust your peepers."

"No dust in my eyes you clod-troll. Can only be a traveller at this time, is there a cardivan?"

"Yes, but short and dull. No sign of gleamy."

"Travellers never show gleamy if they have it or no. Always play pauper."

"Ah, but we may have luckyluck this time."

"Why, what do you see?"

"Another."

"Another traveller?"

"No, one traveller, one panion, smaller, small, snipegut."

"Snipegut? Padding to culport? Non permitted."

"Yes, non permitted, except a traveller …"

"May pass with any cargo."

"Xacly, and only one reason a traveller would sport a snipegut."

"Gleamy!"

"Gleamy. So if traveller has gleamy from snipegut …?"

"He can shed a little for the orphan fund."

"Surely must. And would snipegut give all gleamy to traveller?"

"Snipegut need gleamy for journey."

"Xacly, so maybe twotime luckyluck for us poor orphans."

"Time to twinlock culport door-to-beyond and power up big-voice."

"Don't forget ragflap on iris camvid."

"Getting ragflap now, I keep it under rattletin – gleamy, gleamy, gleamy; rattle, rattle, rattle."

"Just make sure we are ready, we've had a small pickings so much catch-up to do."

"Gleamy, gleamy gleamy; rattle, rattle, rattle: gleamy, gleamy, gleamy; rattle, rattle, rattle ….."

Missed Steps

Are all stepladders laddies
are there lady ladders too
or when you step inside love
do you find they're gender neutral?

Step on, step back, step up, step wild
born to step out as a Steppenwolf child
club step, cub step, rub-a-dub dub step
sidestep, high-step, bi-step, my step

Does Jacob's cracker ladder
run to heaven in your stocking
when there's no room at the instep
for a soul who's just hopscotching?

fast step, mass step, steps of toughened glass
quick step, slip step, don't step on the grass
doorstep, floor step, raw step, war step
first step, nursed step, cursed step, worst step

Should we find a girl to love
step one from Eddie Cochran
or is this total Madness
one step beyond bed notching

step aside, one step ahead, watch your witch step lame
step into the groove, step time, to step up your game
two step, goose step, Led Stairway to balloon step
goon step, doom step, giant leaping moon step

Comfy on the miss step
let's step up to the plate
no false step on any toes
step change don't step away

hop step, stop step, Steptoe and Son
hot step, shot step, stepson of a gun
step over, step forward, baby step into the car
don't step down, don't step off, don't take that step too far.

Blew

Rhubarb
Celery
Wood
Glue
All sticks
Not all do
You did
Like dynamite

Leaving

Surrounded by wild ribbons foaming white on blue and grey
separated islands you may think have had their day
peopled by a mongrel race with far too much to say
beating chests in white string vests dressed ready for the fray
Come what, May?

Pendulum has swung against the clan that dared to play
Cameron has come and gone down Referendum Way
political disillusion now the ordered feet of clay
retuning to old customs "Can you prove your right to stay?"
Johnson's Chez?

Undermined foundations rattle teacups on the tray
Boris World slap happy until they feel the City sway
still exit is the only sign no-one allowed to stray
cut off our nose to spite our face hear those donkeys bray
Leaving? Hey!

Smart Mouth Smart

Working each dark passage
cruise control on cute one liners
emphasise their meaning
with a red ink underliner
poet parrot fashion
just a rhymer not a miner
every which word,
know one choosing it.

Sixty-seven stories
once upon a flaw
can't tell what I'm thinking
even seconds split before
pleasant and revolting
keep revolving door to door
everybody's
always doing it.

Superfluous to the present
like a box kept in the loft
Rapunzel hairpeace pinned beneath
a cap that's never doffed
mint in chocolate coffin
soggy centre supersoft
you might find that
I am losing it.

See me on the catwalk
wearing Yves St Laurent
my modelling behaviour
earns a waiver from the don
you're only semi-naked
if you keep your knickers on
loose elastic
who's been chewing it?

My smart mouth
leaves me smarting
my fast lip
curl is cruel
my pout's more
barbed than Barbie
my trap leaves
me to hang.

A Sticky Situation (apologies to Lear)

My stick insect's got a sulk on.
One of those big ones,
so heavy it hunches your shoulders,
compresses your neck,
furrows your brow
and bloats your bottom lip.
Her face is turned away
so she cannot see
the entreaty in my eyes,
my come hither smile
or hear my unrequited sigh
in softly spoken verse:
"Oh lovely Sticky! Oh Sticky, my love,
What a beautiful Sticky you are,
You are,
You are!
What a beautiful Sticky you are!"
Resolutely sullen
she presents only her back,
ignores the gentle caress
of my delicate touch,
unmoved and unmoving.
My resolve is equally stubborn,
hour after hour
the stroke of my finger,
soliloquy of tongue,
pursed lips rich with kisses,
awaiting the moon
and a hillside Turkey
to wed us.

"Oh lovely Sticky! Oh Sticky, my love."
In your stillness I have hope,
in your silence, longing,
in our night, the comfort of dark.
Morning dawns like lightning
a flash of lasered truth
that my hours were whiled alone
you long flown
and I am left
bereft
with a stick.

Ill Wind III

You can't get khaki car keys
but you can get a khaki car key holder
I lost my duck key
now my Khaki Campbell won't quack
it seems my luck took a plunge
with a clockwork duck a l'orange.

You cannot be serious in cerise
but you can get cereals in series
CoCo Pops through Cornflakes to Rice Crispies
but you said my variety pack
has lost its crackle and popped its snap
little wonder my Khaki Campbell won't quack!

Are you sure you're assured in azure
I'm ensured you can get too cocksure
so insure I implore as you're heading offshore
if you drown then for sure I'll be blue
but although I'll be sore I at least won't be poor
and might learn what too cocksure can do!

Curtailed by Lips

You wish for a butterfly tongue
intent on tasting the depth of ecstasy.
Instead it flaps, trapped
in your mouth for a fortnight,
then crumbles to powder,
dusts away on your cough.

You wish for gleaming teeth
to beguile a sparkle smile
and rive your enemies.
Instead they mirror the sun,
blind your friends,
incinerate your lovers.

You wish for a golden voice
to weight your words,
gild your motifs, enrich your oratory.
Instead your utterance is melted to ingots,
buried beneath pyramids,
vaulted from society.

You wish for the breath of life,
a reviving kiss scented with immortality.
Instead you diffuse contagion,
blow whisps of destruction,
exhale diseased winds of death,
until you beg your lips be stitched.

Eno's Nose

Brian Eno's nose
has holes that drip
on Brian Eno's toes
unless he's wearing
Brian Eno's clothes,
in outer space
or upside down.

Brian Eno knows
his nose has holes
that drip upon his toes
unless he's wearing
Brian Eno's clothes,
in outer space
or upside down.

Sometimes Brian Eno
shows he knows
his nose has holes
that drip upon his toes
unless he's wearing
Brian Eno's clothes,
in outer space
or upside down.

Brian Eno's socks
have lots of spots
of snot that got
there from the holes
in Brian Eno's nose
while wearing clothes
but not
in outer space
or upside down.

Brian Eno and his nose
eventually came to blows
which brought the matter
to a close
though no-one ever
asked his toes.

Committed

The worst sins
are committed in the name of God
religion gives power to the evil sod
while the earth is dying do you find it odd
that the worst sins
are committed in the name of God.

We plough on
as if the clay can rule the clod
follow in the same steps forbears trod
with a sly wink and an almost imperceptible nod
the worst sins
are committed in the name of God.

The moon beams
on the advance military squad
trench feet march to a jungle ipod
affixing bayonets to give the sleeping a prod
the worst sins
are committed in the name of God.

A back breaks
from too many bricks in the hod
no rights, keep quiet just do your job
you get to feed you family we get to make a wad
the worst sins
are committed in the name of God.

Vicars and priests
from every holy synod
glory in their holes don't spare the rod
swing their incense hide amongst the fog
the worst sins
are committed in the name of God.

Social media
has the brain of a brachiopod
caught on the tidal flow and swept along
it's a quick click from community to an angry mob
the worst sins
are committed in the name of God.
Amen.

Starling

Didn't think this time would come,
should I have known, flown home
Can't turn back just one way to go, so slow
There's no use playin' down what's in your soul
"Back to your hole," they said
Then the string kings removed their shades, raised plays
Made out like there's no choice
laid their Ace of Spades, blades graze
Don't push the eject, we might not come down alive
I'm a starling murmuring alone
sing out but no-one hears me
such a waste of space and time
Just a starling weightless in the sky
I try hard not to show it
Hide the fear deep down inside
It scolds me
We know you're a loser
All know you're a loser
Always will be a loser
Wish I had known someone I could've played the fool to too
Say, you're not here, still I hear your new crew flew
Perched on the sofa we can peck out all our plumes for glue
Never a winner, I don't have the fight, might, right
But if I speak up, will you be my bright, white knight
Will I find courage be forever locked up by fright
I'm a starling murmuring alone
sing out but no-one hears me
such a waste of space and time
Just a starling weightless in the sky
I try hard not to show it
But my fear is on the rise
It scolds me
We know you're a loser
All know you're a loser
Always will feel a loser

Myplace

"Can I come with you?"

"You don't know where I'm going."

"Yes I do!"

"(laughs) So where might that be?"

"Away."

"Away where?"

"Away from here."

"And what's so bad about here?"

"Here is neither bad nor good. It is nothing, that's what's so awful about it."

"What makes you think 'there' is better?"

"It will be something. And, there will be the journey."

"So it is journeying you're after?"

"Change."

"Even a change for the worse?"

"If it is too terrible, there can be another journey, and then another."

"What if you can never stop?"

"I will stop."

"When, where?"

"When I find myplace."

"I see. It is true, everyone has to find their place, but what if your place is here?"

"I admit that may be possible, but it is not 'now!'"

"Ah, there is always 'now' and 'not now', here or there."

"Can I come with you?"

"Now?"

"Yes."

"Yes."

Notes

'More Scarecrow Than Pirate' confesses my failure to stand up and be counted.

'Lost Without a Trace' playfully contains eleven trace elements and grew from a seed planted in my early teens when I saw the comedy western *The Brothers O'Toole*. Directed by Richard Erdman, the film is set in the fictitious tumbledown Colorado town of Molybedume, pronounced by the locals as "Molly Be Damned".

'Prince Pince Nez' written on the renaming of the Second Severn Crossing.

'Ysbryd Bywyd' was first performed in February 2024 as a song at the 80th birthday of Dilys Jones in Aberaeron Memorial Hall, the occasion also serving as a fundraiser for Ceredigion's turn as host county for the Royal Welsh Show. Dilys, who has deep family connections to the show, both commissioned the song and inspired its content. My Welsh attracts justifiable correction and criticism, although I do try to twist rather than mangle the language and there are some words here specific to Ceredigion and the Teifi Valley.

'Spirit of Life' is my own translation of 'Ysbryd Bywyd'.

'Truth Hole' draws on the traditional magpie nursery rhyme 'One for Sorrow, Two for Joy' where "seven is a secret never to be told".

'Old Money' was conceived on receiving the first coin bearing the new king's head at the bookshop.

'Crematory Clowns (Advertisement)' arrived a few days after officiating at my mother-in-law's funeral.

'That's Something': I loved Farley's Rusks and ate them well into my teens. Charley Farley is a fictional detective played by Ronnie Corbett, assistant to Piggy Malone played by Ronnie Barker. A regular skit in the 1970s 'Two Ronnies' comedy series, it has one of the best detective theme tunes ever.

'A Meeting of Caterpillars': I once took my mother to the Savoy for afternoon tea and thought "It's also a cabbage".

'Whirled Peas' was inspired by the Leonard Cohen song 'Bird on the Wire'.

'Bug Love': Rubiales' kiss of Hermoso after the 2023 Women's World Cup Final gave new meaning to the "touching hands" lyric of the England team's unofficial anthem 'Sweet Caroline' by Neil Diamond. I then learned that the Giant Amoeba's Latin name is *Chaos carolinense*.

'Lime Regis' contains 31 citrus fruits, several more citrus references and possibly half a line stolen from Max Boyce.

'Cause for Crows': Ænima is a groundbreaking album by art rock band Tool.

'Lash' appeared during a workshop with Menna Elfyn at St David's University College Lampeter in February 2025 and draws on a childhood experience.

'Grannell': On graduating from the Welsh Agricultural College, Aberystwyth, Niki and I moved to Glyn Yr Helyg, Gorsgoch on 31 October 1983. We left for Aberaeron on 28 April 2023 and the new owners kindly allowed me a last walk around the farm on 12 June 2023. Sitting by the river, twiddling in my fingers two feathers discarded by resident buzzards, I sobbed my goodbyes as these lines floated into my head. A tributary of the Teifi, the Grannell is regularly used to convey sewage from the Cribyn outfall *https://www.floodmapper.co.uk/stations/cso-at-cribyn-wwtw-ceredigion-cribyn*.

'Examination' is an updated version of a childhood poem written during my French CSE exam.

'Wondering': I wonder.

'Haicukoo' was written on International Haiku Day 17 April 2024.

'Shoe Kazoo': Lover's Bridge is a local name for the footbridge upstream from the road bridge over the Aeron at Aberaeron. Drill and trap are sub-genres of hip-hop music; all make use of a booming bass sound originally delivered by a Roland TR-808 drum machine. PiL stands for Public Image Limited, a group fronted by ex-Sex Pistol John Lydon which was signed to Richard Branson's Virgin record label. Twm Sion Catti is a 16th century highwayman sometimes called the Welsh Robin Hood.

'Piggy Bop' was inspired by Iggy Pop..

'Owl and Dove' resulted from a workshop with Menna Elfyn at St David's University College Lampeter in February 2025 and a sharing of objects with poet Jaqi Sandover. The letter J was added to the Welsh alphabet in 1987. There is no letter V as this sound is signified by a single F. *Duende* is a Spanish word meaning a heightened emotional response to an artistic performance or object.

'Culporter Conspiracy': One for the Gleamy…

'A Sticky Situation' draws from Edward Lear's 'The Owl and the Pussycat'.

'Ill Wind III': Swansea clubbers will know how this is pronounced.

'Starling' was inspired by David Bowie.

Acknowledgements

I must first express my gratitude to my editor John Eliot and publisher Chuck Grieve, both for the release of work through Mosaïque Press and for their patience and professionalism. I try to call all the shots, from fonts and full stops to cover images and positioning of titles, but appreciate their knowledge, experience and gentle steerage to the collection you hold in your hand. To Geraint Lewis for his wonderful Foreword, support, encouragement, humour and patience with my Welsh.

To the editors, promoters and artists who have supported my development as a writer and performer and shaped and encouraged my output: Menna Elfyn, Gillian Clarke, Rufus Mufasa, Jackie Biggs, Dominic Williams, Michael Kennedy, Dave Urwin, Eliza Filimon, Mike Jenkins, Robert Minhinnick, Kaysha Louvain, Kathy Miles, Rebecca Lowe, Sue Moules, Carly Holmes, Steve Greenhalgh, John Collins, Daria Limatola, Mel Perry, Dilys Jones, Nahal Namvari, Rhoda Thomas, Freya Blyth, Linda Barone, Lazarus Carpenter and important people I've inadvertently omitted.

To fellow members of WordPlay Collective: Annie Butler, Paul Hayes, Paul Steffan Jones, Richard Wheeler and Cecile Cailleau, your invitation and camaraderie are invaluable.

To fellow members of Lampeter Writers' Workshop and Cardigan's Cellar Bards for their critical havens where everything gets tested; Literature Wales for supporting my performances; Tiwn Media for the breaks; and Equity my Trade Union.

To Niki, my wife and everything, and the rest of the Cairngorm Five, Pat, Steph and Nicola.

KGB
Aberaeron, March 2025